Galen Norman

473 Words to Inspire, Educate and Entertain

Discover unusual and long-forgotten words to improve your English vocabulary and increase your love of the English language

This book was professionally typeset on Reedsy
Find out more at reedsy.com

Contents

   1.

   2.

   3.

   4.

   5.

   6.

   7.

   8.

   9.

   10.

   11.

   12.

   13.

   14.

   15.

   16.

   17.

   18.

   19.

   20.

21.

22.

23.

24.

25.

26.

27.

28.

29.

30.

31.

32.

33.

34.

35.

36.

37.

38.

39.

40.

41.

Introduction

Are you looking to expand your vocabulary, but don't want to spend hours searching through dictionaries? Look no further.

We have done the hard work for you and found these 473 words that will brighten your day, spread some love and happiness and improve your English language skills.

This pocket-sized book is unlike a traditional dictionary. It is organised into easy-to-find topics so you can find the exact word for that specific situation easily and quickly.

Whether you are a book lover, a word enthusiast or just looking to impress someone special, this book is full of words that will make you tingle with 'linguosity' (taking pleasure in words). I've tried not to 'be scribacious' (write too much) and only included the key facts and origins where it aids understanding.

- Struggling to find the precise word to use in a situation?
- Bored of saying the same old phrases and words?
- Looking to impress someone special?
- Keen to keep lesser-spotted words going?
- Want to find new words to stretch your vocabulary?

Let me help you expand your vocabulary with 473 of the more unusual, under-used and unfamiliar words in the English language. Some of these words are long-forgotten gems. A few of these words have simply fallen out of use.

All of these words will inform, educate and entertain and will add much-needed 'Zhuzh' to your conversations.

So   let's   dive   in...

Animals

Desticate: *Noun*
> To cry or squeak like a rat.

Dew Snail: *Noun*
> An unusual name for a slug.

Rhinarium: *Noun*
> The moist nose of an animal (like a dog or cat).

Skirr: *Verb*
> The sound of birds' wings in flight.

Winx: *Noun*
> To bray like a donkey.

Argument & Debate

Brabble: *Verb*
A noisy argument over things that don't matter.

Cromulent: *Noun*
Genuine or acceptable.

Escarmouche: *Noun*
A brief disagreement or argument.

Fratchy: *Noun*
Argumentative and short-tempered.

Gymnologise: *Noun*
Having a naked argument.

Ipsidexitist: *Noun*
When someone asserts a fact, but they do not have any supporting evidence to support their claim.

Jawbation: *Noun*
An extensive scolding.

Mumpsimus: *Noun*
A stubborn person who still clings to their beliefs even though their beliefs are proved to be incorrect.

Paralipsis: *Noun*
A rhetorical device where you emphasize the idea by not saying anything about it.

Philodox: *Noun*

Someone who is in love with their own opinion. They believe everyone else should share their opinion.

Quodlibertarian: *Noun*

A pedantic blowhard; someone who argues over every single point.

Ratiocinator: *Noun*

The word to describe someone who reasons logically and methodically.

Recumbentibus: *Noun*

Delivering a knockdown punch.

Sockdolager: *Noun*

The decisive winning point in an argument or debate that settles it.

Swasivious: *Noun*

Persuasion   in   an   agreeable   way.

Books

Biblioklept: *Noun*

The name for a book thief; someone who borrows a book and never gives it back.

Lectory: *Noun*

A quiet place for reading.

Lucubration: *Noun*

The nocturnal study, writing or meditation.

Vellichor: *Noun*

The smell of old books and the feelings it evokes.

Clothing

Apple-catchers: *Noun*
A large pair of pants or knickers.

Cover-slut: *Noun*
An item of clothing is deliberately worn on top of a stained item of clothing so no one can see the unsightly stain.

Flamfoo: *Noun*
A flamboyantly-dressed person who is more fizz than substance.

Flype: *Noun*
Roll your socks up and then put them on.

Huffle-buffs: *Noun*
Old or comfortable clothes you can't wait to get into (and stay in all day).

Nickerers: *Noun*
That creaking sound new shoes make when you first walk in them.

Shivviness: *Noun*
That strange and uncomfortable feeling when you wear new underwear for the first time.

Trumperiness: *Noun*
Something that is flashy and showy but is ultimately worthless.

Confusion

Bumfuzzle: *Verb*
To confuse or perplex.

Doggerybaw: *Noun*
Nonsense. Gibberish.

Fratchy: *Adjective*
Argumentative. Irritable and quarrelsome.

Skimble-Skamble: *Adjective*
Confused. Rambling.

Widdim / Widdendream: *Noun*
A mad fit. Mental confusion or excitement.

Deceit

Hookem-snivy: *Noun*
Trickery or deceit.

Illywhacker: *Noun*
A confidence trickster.

Pseudologist: *Noun*
Someone who lies.

Snollygoster: *Noun*
A dishonest and unprincipled person in public office.

Drink

Bibulous: *Adjective*
Someone very fond of alcoholic beverages.

Bitching the pot: *Noun*
Victorian slang for pouring the tea out of a teapot.

Cherubimical: *Noun*
A happy drunk, first used by Benjamin Franklin.

Drowning the Miller: *Noun*
An old Royal Navy term to describe when you use more water than necessary.

Dutch-Feast: *Idiom*
When the host of a party gets drunk before the guests.

Jack brew: *Noun*

Military slang for when you make a cuppa for yourself and don't ask anyone else. As in "I'm alright Jack".

Jirble: *Verb*

When your hands are shaking so you pour carelessly and spill a liquid.

Lanspresado: *Noun*

The name to describe the person who has "accidentally" forgotten their wallet or purse.

Lick-spigot: *Noun*

The name of that friend who is always there whenever they hear a cork popping.

Merry-go-down: *Noun*

A strong ale or beer.

Neckum, Swinkum, Swankum: *Noun*

The three different draughts you can pour from one keg of ale.

Nepenthe: *Noun*

A drink, potion or drug used by the ancients that were thought to bring forgetfulness of all painful worries, altering your state of mind for the better.

Nuncheon: *Noun*

A light mid-morning or mid-afternoon snack of cheese, bread and beer.

Potpanion: *Noun*

A drinking companion.

Spumescent: *Adjective*

Frothy or foamlike.

Terroir: *Noun*

In native French this means 'soil' and is a concept in winemaking to describe the factors – the climate, the soil, the environment – that combine to give wines their particular character.

Thermopot: *Noun*

18th Century word for someone who drinks a lot of hot drinks.

Tosspot: *Noun*

Name for alcoholic drinkers who tossed back their bottle of beer.

Xertz: *Noun*

To gulp a liquid down quickly.

Zarf: *Noun*

A tube-shaped holder for a coffee cup (e.g. the cardboard sleeve   is   a   zarf).

Feelings

Atrabilious: *Adjective*
Melancholy: to be sullen or bad-tempered.

Betwitterment *Noun*
Nervous. Excited. Fearful.

Confelicity: *Noun*
Finding joy in someone else's happiness (the opposite of schadenfreude).

Dander: *Noun*
Feeling cross.

Dumfungled: *Adjective*
When you feel drained and exhausted.

Fellowfeel: *Verb*
  To empathize, to have empathy.

Finnying: *Noun*
  Feeling fearful or timid.

Gloppenment: *Noun*
  A surprising feeling of astonishment.

Kvell / Kvelling: *Verb*

To be very proud; bursting with pride or satisfaction.

Quakebuttock: *Noun*

An old-fashioned term for a coward.

Twazziness: *Noun*

When you feel bad-tempered, snappy or grumpy.

Food

Alliaceous: *Noun*
To describe a garlic or onion smell or taste.

Bags of mystery: *Noun*
Old English slang for sausages as you didn't know what was in them.

Bedinner: *Verb*
To give someone dinner.

Bedinnered: *Verb*
To be served dinner by someone else.

Biffin: *Noun*
A deep-red cooking apple.

Bouffage: *Noun*
The name for a delicious and enjoyable slap-up meal.

Brakish: *Adjective*
Used to describe slightly salty water.

Browjans: *Noun*
A Cornish expression for crumbs or fragments of food.

Claggy: *Adjective*
Describes food that forms clots and has a sticky texture.

Conflagrant: *Adjective*
On fire – a hot pepper sensation.

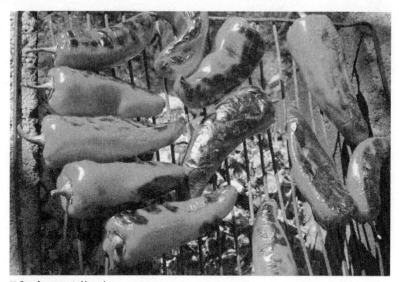

Edacious: *Adjective*
Being very fond of eating.

Fire-Fanged: *Verb*
Food that is overcooked or dry and has a seared appearance and taste.

Friable: *Adjective*
Food that is easily crumbled or pulverized, like short-crust pastry, in your fingers.

Gloppy: *Noun*
An unattractive substance that has a half solid, half liquid consistency.

Groke / Groaking: *Noun*
This old Scottish word describes how dogs longingly gaze and salivate at food in the hope you may share it with them.

Guddle: *Noun*

Another old Scottish term for fishing with one's hands instead of a fishing rod.

Hogo: *Noun*

A notably strong aroma or smell. From the French 'Haut goût', or highly seasoned.

Jentacular: *Adjective*

Eating breakfast as soon as you get out of bed, early in the morning.

Medulline: *Noun*

The soft pulp of a fruit: the pith.

Mordacious: *Adjective*

Food with a bite or kick. Can also be used to describe a caustic and corrosive style.

Neptunian: *Noun*
Relates to the Roman Sea God Neptune and describes the salty character of food from the sea.

Nidorosity: *Noun*
A disgusting belch that smells of undigested meat.

Nippitatum: Noun
Long-forgotten term to describe a strong alcoholic drink.

Opulent: *Adjective*
Extravagant luxury.

Ortanique: Noun
A citrus fruit that is a cross between an orange and a tangerine.

Pertish: *Adjective*
A food with a bold flavour or kick.

Pica: *Noun*
The craving to eat unusual food is particularly experienced during pregnancy.

Pingle: *Verb*
When you fiddle with or pick at your food.

Pinguid: *Adjective*
Oily or greasy.

Pumpernickel: *Noun*
The German rye bread also means a farting demon.

Shotclog: *Noun*

A pub companion (**Potpanion**) who you put up with because they are buying the next round of drinks.

Slabsauce: *Noun*

A person who appreciates eating fine food.

Slape: *Adjective*

A rich, sugary taste.

Snap: *Noun*

An old-fashioned term for dinner. Comes from when miners used to carry a tin box which snapped open and closed at mealtimes.

Suaveolent: *Adjective*

Sweet-scented. Fragrant.

Tachyphagia: *Noun*

Bolting down food; eating very quickly.

Tostada: *Noun*

Spanish / Mexican in origin, this translates as 'toasted' in English. It is a deep-fried tortilla, topped with cheese, meat and refried beans.

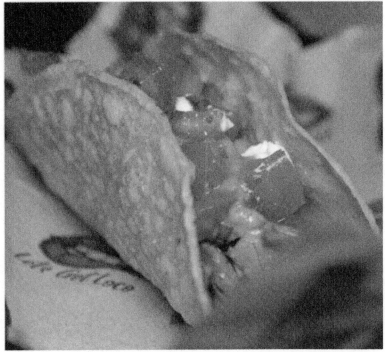

Tremulous: *Adjective*

The quivering and shaking of jelly are tremulous.

Geography

Abyssal: *Noun*

The darkest and deepest parts of the Ocean (between 3,000 and 6,000 metres deep).

Dub: *Noun*

An old Scottish and Northern word for a pool of stagnant water.

Mere: *Noun*

A broad but not deep lake.

Pulk: *Noun*

From the Northern dialect for a mudhole or standing water.

Quag: *Noun*

A shortened version of a quagmire. A marsh or bog, where the ground is soft and flabby.

Happiness

Confelicity: *Noun*
Means taking joy in other people's happiness.

Forblissed: *Noun*
Full of happiness.

Grinagog: *Noun*
That person who is always cheerful no matter what.

Gigglemug: *Noun*
Someone who is permanently cheerful.

Goshbustified: *Noun*
To be excessively pleased.

Hate

Flarnecking: *Noun*

The flaunting of success by someone you don't like.

Interdespise: *Verb*

To   hate   someone   as   much   as   they   hate   you.

History

January: *Noun*
Named after Janus, the ancient Roman God of doors and new beginnings.

Madeleine: *Noun*
The rich, shell-shaped French cake was named after Mary Magdalene.

Sarcophagus: *Noun*

A limestone tomb or coffin that gradually decomposed the body buried within it.

Swansong: *Noun*

The final performance. The ancient belief was that swans were born mute (untrue) and remained mute until the moment of death when they sing a mournful song.

Home

Aflunters *Adverb*
In a state of mess and disorder.

Fossick: *Verb*
To search and rummage around.

Growlery: *Noun*
The place you retreat to when you're feeling unwell or ill-humoured. Charles Dickens coined 'Growlery' in his novel Bleak House.

Half-pace: *Noun*
A small landing between two half flights in a staircase.

Introuvable: *Adjective*
Incapable of being found, specifically books and pamphlets.

Nidificate: *Verb*
To build a nest.

Scurryfunge: *Verb*
That mad dash to tidy the house up just before visitors arrive.

Language

Bafflegab: *Noun*
Jargon, especially bureaucratic & incomprehensible that confuses instead of clarifying.

Battology: *Adjective*
Repetition, relentlessly repeating the same thing over and over and over again.

Haplology: *Noun*
The leaving out of one occurrence of a syllable or sound that is (probly) repeated in a word (e.g. probably).

Linguosity: *Noun*
Taking pleasure in using words (maybe a little too much!).

Milver: *Noun*
Someone with whom one shares an interest in words and wordplay.

Paralipsis: *Noun*
The rhetorical device of emphasizing the subject by saying little or nothing about the subject.

Paraph: *Noun*
The flourish after a written signature (originated as a precaution against forgery).

Prepone: *Verb*
The antonym to postpone. To bring something forward in time.

Psittacism: *Noun*
Mechanical or meaningless repetition of words and phrases.

Salvo: *Noun*
A deliberately bad excuse.

Scribacious: *Adjective*
Prone to writing a lot or too much.

Sesquipedalian: *Adjective*
Polysyllabic words are sesquipedalian as they have too many syllables. Can also mean characterized by too many long words.

Stultiloquence: *Noun*
Senseless or foolish talk or babble.

Tittle: *Noun*

The dot above the letter i or j is a tittle.

Tmesis: *Noun*

Dividing one word by up butting another in the middle. e.g. 'abso-bloody-lutely'.

Laughter

Cachinnator: *Noun*

Someone who laughs too loudly.

Snirtle: *Verb*

Scottish for a snigger. When you try to suppress your laughter (often without success).

Witzelsucht: *Noun*

A tendency of telling poor jokes. A feeble attempt at humour.

Local Dialects

Capadocious: *Adjective*
Spoken in Devon or Yorkshire, meaning excellent or splendid.

Flinterkin: *Noun*
From Orkney to describe a dry cow pat.

Glimmer-gowk: *Noun*
First used by Alfred Tennyson to describe an owl in Gloucestershire and Lincolnshire.

Kiddlywink: *Noun*
An old Cornish word for a small pub
or ale house.

Lagom: *Noun*
(Swedish) Not too much or too little but just the right amount.

Moonraker: *Noun*
A native of the county of Wiltshire.

Pana po'o: *Verb*
Hawaiian word means to scratch your head to help you remember something you have forgotten.

Poppinoddles: *Noun*
A Cumbrian term for a somersault.

Poronkusema: *Noun*

Finnish for reindeer urine. It is a Finnish measurement based on the distance a reindeer can travel before needing a comfort break.

Strolloping: *Verb*

An old Lancashire verb for going out in a scruffy, slovenly manner.

Twickered: *Adjective*

From the Isle of Wight meaning tired or weary.

Ugsome: *Adjective*

A Viking word means feeling disgust towards someone.

Love

Belgard: *Noun*
A loving look, an amorous glance.

Bovarism: *Noun*
A romanticised perception of oneself.

Concupiscence: *Noun*
Lust. A strong sexual desire.

Consenescence: *Noun*
To grow old together.

Drachenfutter: *Noun*
A gift like chocolate, flowers or treats that one buys to give to their partner to appease them.

Elozable: *Adjective*
Influenced by, and amenable to, flattery.

Engouement: *Noun*
Infatuation and an irrational fondness for something.

Osculable: *Adjective*
Able to be tenderly kissed.

Pigsney: *Noun*
Sweetheart. Darling or beloved.

Puckeration: *Noun*
State of excitement. Anything that gets us hot under the collar

Quixotic: *Adjective*

Quixotic means hopeful and extravagantly romantic but in an unpractical way. It originates from Miguel el de Cervantes' 17th Century novel Don Quixote.

Sardonian: *Adjective*

Flattering with harmful or deadly intent.

Smirting: *Noun*

Flirting   with   someone   while   you're   smoking.

Mental Health

Beblubbed: *Noun*
Swollen eyes from too much crying.

Depooperit: *Adjective*
A state of near imbecility.

Dumfungled: *Adjective*
Worn out.

Fobly-Mobly: *Noun*
18th Century term means neither well nor unwell. A bit 'meh'.

Forplaint: *Adjective*
Exhausted from weeping.

Gowl: *Verb*
Weeping in anger or frustration.

Mardy: *Noun*
Grumpy person. Comes from a spoilt child who misbehaves and becomes grumpy and sulky.

Merry-go-sorry: *Noun*
Feeling a mixture of joy and sadness.

Microlipet: *Noun*
Someone who gets stressed and all worked up about trivial things.

Omnistrain: *Verb*

The stress of trying to cope with everything in life and doing everything at once.

Peely-wally: *Adjective*

Scottish term for feeling rather "meh" or under the weather.

Resipiscence: *Noun*

Returning to a better state of mind.

Respair: *Noun*

A fresh hope. A return to recovery.

Solastalgia: *Noun*

A portmanteau of solace and nostalgia: the physical and emotional stress caused by environmental change.

Wambleropt: *Noun*

A rumbly stomach: feeling decidedly queasy.

Widdrim / Widdendream: *Noun*

To be in a state of confusion or mental excitement.

Woofits: *Noun*

An unwell feeling, especially a headache. Can also be used to describe a moody depression.

Movement

Absquatulate: *Verb*
> To leave in a hurry.

Balter: *Verb*
> To dance clumsily.

Brachiate: *Verb*
> Use your arms to swing from tree branch to tree branch.

Gaincope: *Verb*
> To meet or intercept someone by taking a shortcut.

Hirple: *Verb*
> Scottish word meaning to walk with a limp.

Nuddle: *Verb*
> To walk by yourself with your head held low.

Obambulate: *Verb*
> To wander.

Oxtercog: *Verb*
> Northern Irish term means carry someone by supporting them under the armpits.

Pratfall: *Noun*
> A comedic fall onto your buttocks.

Scuddling: *Verb*
> To run hastily.

Skedaddle: *Verb*

To leave quickly or hurriedly.

Sprunt: *Verb*

A Victorian Scottish word meaning to chase girls and boys around a haystack in the dark.

Striddle: *Verb*

To walk uncomfortably.

Trampoose: *Verb*

To   trudge   and   walk   reluctantly.

Music

Glad-warble: *Verb*
 Singing joyfully.

Doppet: *Verb*
 To jerkily play a musical instrument.

Plangent: *Noun*
 A loud and resonant sound.

Tintinnabulation: *Noun*
 The lingering sound of a ringing bell, after it has been struck.

Twankle: *Verb*
 To idly play on a musical instrument.

People and Personalities

'-sby': *Noun*
A suffix is added to describe a person's character trait. e.g. A rudesby is rude, an idlesby is idle, a sneaksby is sneaky.

Balatronic: *Noun*
The characteristic of a buffoon.

Blandishment: *Noun*
False flattery of someone.

Bloviator: *Noun*
Someone who gives their pompous opinion: a braggot or a boaster.

Blunkerkin: *Noun*
Someone who is generally incompetent.

Boondoggle: *Noun*
An unnecessary or wasteful undertaking.

Carnaptious: *Adjective*
Bad-tempered.

Cockalorum: *Noun*
A self-important man.

Crumpsy: *Noun*
Grumpy and irritable.

Dispester: *Verb*
To get rid of a nuisance or a pest.

Dixiefixie: *Noun*
Being held in a state of confinement.

Dowfart: *Noun*
A dull, stupid or ineffectual person.

Flatigious: *Adjective*
From the 14th Century, to describe someone who is unbelievably evil.

Gollumpus: *Adjective*
A large, clumsy and loutish person.

Gongoozler: *Noun*
A person who likes watching activities of others on the canal network and can mindlessly stare at anything.

Grumbletonian: *Noun*
A person who grumbles often.

Hankersore: *Adjective*
When you find someone else so attractive it pisses you off.

Humgruffin: *Noun*
A 19th-century word for a snarly repulsive person (especially in the morning).

Idiorepulsive: *Adjective*
Self-repelling.

Inadvertist: *Noun*
Someone who consistently fails to notice what is going on around them.

Jettatore: *Noun*
Someone who brings bad luck with them.

Kenspeckle: *Adjective*
Easily recognized or conspicuous.

Leese: *Verb*
To be a loser.

Lobcock: *Noun*
A dull, sluggish person.

Miscounsel: *Verb*
To wrongly advise.

Ne'er-Do-Well: *Noun*
A derogatory term to describe someone you deem to be a bit useless: a good-for-nothing, ineffectual or lazy person.

Nudnik: *Noun*
A nagging, pestering or irritating person; a bore.

Percunctorily: *Noun*
Half-heartedly or negligently.

Philodox: *Noun*
A person in love with their own opinion.

Pronk: *Noun*
A weak or slightly foolish person.

Pronk: *Verb*
To leap in the air like a springbok.

Quidnunc: *Noun*
A gossipy and inquisitive person.

Quockerwodger: *Noun*
A wooden puppet on strings that are controlled by someone else.

Rambunctious: *Adjective*
Exuberant and boisterous.

Rantipole: *Noun*
A wild and reckless young person.

Scrouging: *Verb*
Discomfort someone by standing too close to them.

Shackbaggerly: *Adjective*
Anything left in a disorganized or slovenly manner.

Shoulder-clapper: *Noun*
Someone who is unnecessarily friendly and overfamiliar.

Slubberdegullian: *Noun*
A slob.

Tatterwallop: *Noun*
An untidy or slovenly person.

Throttlebottom: *Noun*
An inept person in public office.

Ultracrepidarian: *Adjective*
A person who shares their judgements and opinions but knows absolutely nothing about the topic.

Wegotist: *Noun*
Someone who overuses the royal 'we'.

Well-woulder: *Noun*

A well-wisher with conditions. Someone who wishes you success, as long as you are not more successful than them.

Performance

Boffola: *Noun*

A funny joke or a line written in the script to get a laugh from the viewer or audience.

Bucklebuster: *Noun*

A line in a play or book or comedy that makes you laugh out loud.

Zany: *Adjective*

Comic performers would accompany a clown or an acrobat and imitate their master's act in a ludicrously awkward way.

Phobias

Abibliophobia: *Noun*
The fear of being without books and having nothing to read.

Coulrophobia: *Noun*
An extreme fear of clowns.

Ochlophobia: *Noun*
An extreme or irrational fear of crowds.

Nyctophobia: *Noun*
An extreme fear of darkness.

Panic: *Noun*
Dates back to the god Pan who hid in the woods and made mysterious noises to frighten travellers as they passed by.

Phrases

Balatronic: *Noun*
About a clown or a buffoon.

Bobbins: *Noun*
Mancunian for rubbish or nonsense.

Cacafuego: *Noun*
A person with a fiery temper.

Cold Turkey: *Noun*
The phrase originates from the belief that coming off something caused you to have goose bumps or turkey flesh.

Déjà vu: *Noun*
The feeling of having encountered something before and being familiar with it.

Flippercanorious: *Noun*
Something extraordinary or blooming impressive.

Gallimaufry: *Noun*
A confused jumble or mess.

Havey-Cavey: *Adjective*
Uncertain or unsure of what you're doing.

Indread: *Noun*
Be constantly in fear or secret inner dread.

Jamais vu: *Noun*

"Never seen" (the antonym of **Déjà vu**); the feeling of never having encountered something despite being familiar with it.

Monodynamic: *Adjective*

Having one talent only.

Nikhedonia: *Noun*

The pleasure of anticipating success or victory.

Nerdle/Nurdle: *Adjective*

The perfect swoosh of toothpaste on a toothpaste advert.

Pluffy: *Adjective*

To be both fat and fluffy.

Podiacide: *Verb*

Shooting yourself in the foot.

Propinquity: *Noun*

Being close to someone or something.

Redeless: *Adjective*

Without counsel. Not knowing what actions to take in an emergency.

Thankworthy: *Adjective*

Worthy of gratitude like a thank you.

Ultracrepidarian: *Adjective*

Somebody who gives opinions on matters way above their knowledge.

Wheem: *Noun*

An old word for pleasant, gentle, or smooth.

Witches' Knickers: *Noun*

Plastic bags stuck in the branches of a tree.

Places

Chawbacon: *Noun*
Name for a country-dweller.

Fernweh: *Noun*
The opposite of homesickness.

Hibernacle: *Noun*
A winter retreat.

Latibulate: *Noun*
To hide in a corner.

Phrontistery: *Noun*
A place for contemplation.

Twitten: *Noun*
A narrow path or alleyway.

Widdershins: *Noun*
A direction opposite to the usual; counter-clockwise or left-handed.

Yonder: *Noun*
A synonym for over there or in the distance.

Relationships

Angel Visit: *Noun*
Catch-up with a friend that's all too rare.

Exfamiliation: *Noun*
Exclusion or separation from one's own family.

Nibbling: *Noun*
An old expression for a Nephew or niece.

Popjoy: *Verb*
To amuse yourself, celebrate or have fun.

Sequaciousness: *Adjective*
The slavish following of someone else, even to extreme ends.

Tartle: *Noun*
When you forget the name of the person you are introducing.

Twindle: *Noun*
Old   dialect   for   a   twin   sibling.

Rivers and Streams

Bang-a-bonk: *Verb*
Old dialect for sitting lazily on a river bank.

Beck: *Noun*
Northern England term for a stony brook.

Bourne: *Noun*
A small, intermittent stream.

Burble: *Noun*
The sound of a small stream as it flows over stones.

Burn: *Noun*
In Scotland and North England, this means a small intermittent stream.

Foss: *Noun*
An Old Norse word for waterfall.

Freshet: *Noun*

When a river or stream overflows and floods due to heavy rain or snow.

Gill / Ghyll: *Noun*

An old Norse word for a ravine and the water flowing through it.

Riparian: *Noun*

Relating to or situated on the banks of a river.

Rill: *Noun*

16th Century term for a small stream.

Slidder: *Noun*

A   hollow   running   down   a   hill.

Sadness

Begrumpled: *Adjective*
Describes the early morning crumpled self: feeling a bit displeased or offended.

Discombobulate: *Noun*
Feeling confused, upset or frustrated.

Glump: *Verb*
Feeling solemn or glum.

Looseleft: *Noun*
The feeling of loss you get when you complete a rood boxset or book.

Mubble-fubbles: *Noun*
16th Century word meaning a sense of impending doom.

Puzzomous: *Adjective*
Disgustingly obsequious and poisonous.

Seeksorrow: *Noun*
One who acts to his detriment, a self-tormentor.

Science

Catacoustics: *Noun*
The science of reflected sounds: Echoes.

Crambazzled: *Adjective*
Looking prematurely aged or rough from drinking.

Darkle: *Verb*
To grow dark.

Dendrology: *Noun*
The scientific study of trees.

Empurple: *Verb*
To make something purple.

Firefang: *Verb*
Overheated or scorched.

Nyctalopia: *Noun*

Poor vision in low light. Night blindness.

Petrichor: *Noun*

The beautiful smell that occurs when rain falls on dry soil.

Pinguescence: *Noun*

The process of becoming fat.

Pooter: *Noun*

A suction bottle for collecting insects and invertebrates.

Psithurism: *Noun*

The whispering of leaves in the wind.

Snit: *Noun*

The glowing part of the candle wick after the wick has blown out.

Zoosemiotics: *Noun*

The study of animal communication.

Sleep

Chums: *Noun*
Another term for chamber mate. Someone you shared your bedroom with.

Clinomania: *Noun*
The desire to stay lying in bed.

Clinophobia: *Noun*
The antonym of Clinomania: a fear of lying down.

Estivate: *Noun*
The antonym to hibernating: animals go into a state of inactivity during the heat of the summer.

Euneirophrenia: *Noun*
The lingering sensation you get after waking from a pleasant dream.

Forwallowed: *Noun*
Used in the 1400s to mean a disrupted night's sleep when you've been tossing and turning all night.

Hurkle-durkle: *Noun*
A Scottish phrase meaning to lounge in bed long after it was time to get up.

Hypnopompic: *Noun*
That state of consciousness between sleeping and waking.

Nuddle: *Verb*
To walk in a daydreamy state with your head down.

Sloom: *Noun*
From Middle English slumen, meaning to lightly slumber or gently sleep.

Somnificator: *Noun*
A person who induces sleep in someone else.

Uhtceare: *Noun*
To anxiously lie awake just before dawn breaks.

Zwoddery: *Noun*
An old Somerset word for feeling drowsy and almost stupified.

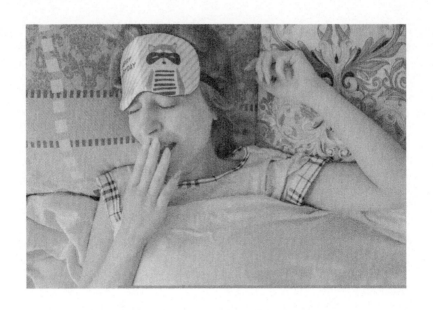

Stupidity

Gove: *Verb*
To stare stupidly.

Parvanimity: *Noun*
Having a little mind or being small-minded.

Princock: *Noun*
A foolish and conceited person.

Quignogs: *Noun*
An old Cornish term for ridiculous ideas or conceits.

Rogitation: *Noun*
To ask the same question over and over again.

Sumph: *Noun*
A   soft,   stupid   fellow.

Talk

Blatteroon: *Noun*
Someone who babbles nonsense.

Conjubilant: *Adjective*
Shouting and rejoicing with others.

Controuver: *Noun*
A person who creates false gossip.

Dentiloquy: *Noun*
The habit of talking through clenched teeth.

Explaterate: *Verb*
To talk continuously without stopping.

Nix: *Verb*
An instruction to stop talking because someone is coming.

Nod-crafty: *Noun*
A person who stopped listening to you, but still nods along with an air of wisdom.

Oxyphonia: *Noun*
Excessive shrillness and high pitch of voice.

Pleep: *Noun*
To speak in a critical tone of voice.

Polylogise: *Noun*
Talking too much.

Quonking: *Noun*

Annoying noises from the sideline.

Siffilate: *Noun*

To speak in a whisper.

Snoaching: *Verb*

To speak through the nose.

Soutband: *Noun*

Someone who deliberately interrupts conversations and constantly corrects and/or contradicts you.

Tacenda: *Noun*

Things that you must not speak about.

Testiculating: *Verb*

To talk bollocks while waving your hands around.

Toot-Moot: *Noun*

A muffled, low conversation between people.

The Body

Acnestis: *Noun*
The part of your back that you can't reach to scratch.

Borborygmus: *Noun*
When gas and fluids are gurgling in your intestines and your stomach grumbles.

Grog-blossom: *Noun*
The veins on your nose are caused by too much drinking of alcohol.

Hopper-arsed: *Noun*
Having large buttocks.

Horripilation: *Noun*
The scientific name for goosebumps is when your hairs stand up on your body.

Humdudgeon: *Noun*
An imaginary illness that may prevent you from getting out of bed or through the office door.

Kwashiorkor: *Noun*
A severe form of malnutrition.

Lalochezia: *Noun*
The relief of tension in your body through swearing.

Leper Juice: *Noun*

A long-forgotten repulsive medical term that refers to the pus found in wounds.

Obdormition: *Noun*

The scientific name for when a limb "goes to sleep" and feels numb.

Pandiculating: *Verb*

Stretching and yawning at the same time.

Paresthesia: *Noun*

The scientific name for pins and needles felt in limbs.

Pilgarlic: *Noun*

A hairless or bald-headed man.

Quobbled: *Noun*

To have wrinkled fingers.

Trullibubs: *Noun*

The entrails of a person. It's also an insulting term for a person who is overweight.

Thorough-cough: *Verb*

When you cough and break wind at the same time.

Urtication: *Noun*

The act of whipping a numb limb with nettles to restore its feelings.

Wamblecropt: *Noun*

Overcome with indigestion and be unable to move due to digestive   issues.

Things

Bilbo: *Noun*
Sword of extraordinary quality used in former times.

Bowerbird: *Noun*
A collector of useless objects or knick-knacks.

Bumbershoot: *Noun*
A Victorian word for an umbrella.

Cackletub: *Noun*
English slang term for a church pulpit.

Chatoyant: *Adjective*
Like a gem that is shimmering iridescent light - a cat's eye in the dark.

Croggy: *Noun*
Get a ride on the handlebars of your friend's bike.

Deliquesce: *Verb*
To melt away or gradually dissolve.

Fandangle: *Noun*
An extravagantly fanciful but useless ornament.

Filipendulous: *Adjective*
Suspended by a thread.

Finagle: *Verb*
To obtain something by dishonest or devious methods.

Finifugal: *Adjective*
Shunning the end of something.

Gowpen: *Noun*
Two handfuls of something; using your hands to make a bowl.

Gubbins: *Noun*
An informal word for bits and pieces.

Knick-knackatarian: *Noun*
A dealer in knick-knacks.

Imbroglio: *Noun*
A complicated and confusing situation.

Insordescent: *Adjective*
Growing in filthiness.

Lubberland: *Noun*
A mythical paradise reserved for those who are lazy.

Maculate: *Adjective*
Stained (antonym to immaculate).

Maverick: Noun
Unorthodox or independent-minded individual. Named after Samuel Augustus Maverick, who left his herd of cattle unbranded.

Mush Faker: *Noun*
Victorian slang for an umbrella repairer.

Pollicitation: *Noun*
An offer made but not yet accepted.

Quisquilious: *Noun*
Worthless and trivial. The nature of rubbish and refuse.

Recrudescence: *Noun*
A new outbreak of an undesirable condition.

Resistentialism: *Noun*
The theory is that inanimate objects display seemingly spiteful behaviour towards their owners.

Solander: *Noun*
A protective box-shaped in the form of a book.

Toe-cover: *Noun*
A cheap and useless present.

Tranklements: *Noun*
A Black Country word for bric-a-brac.

Umbriferous: *Adjective*
Making or casting shade.

Videnda: *Noun*
Things worth seeing.

Vizzying-hole: *Noun*
A delightful Scottish word for a peephole in a door.

Waff: *Verb*
A slight blow; a tiny touch of illness; a glimpse; a waft of perfume; a regal wave.

Zhuzh: *Verb*

To make it more exciting or attractive; add a certain 'je ne sais quoi'.

Weather

Apricity: *Noun*
The warmth of the sun in winter.

Beek/Beeking: *Verb*
To bask in the sunshine or the warmth of the log fire.

Beggars' Velvet: *Noun*
Particles of fine dust floating in the sunlight.

Blunk: *Noun*
A sudden rain storm.

Dreich: *Noun*
A Scottish word for a misty, bleak, damp and dreary day.

Foundered: *Noun*
The Irish word for windblown.

Fulminous: *Adjective*
Word relating to or resembling thunder and lightning.

Haar: *Noun*
A word from Edinburgh to describe the sea fog in the East of Scotland.

Heller: *Noun*
An old term for an intensely cold winter's day when you can no longer feel your hands.

Kelsher / Kelshed: *Noun*
An obscure word from the South West of England means getting caught in a downpour.

Latibulate: *Verb*
Hiding in a warm, cosy corner.

Mafted: *Adjective*
Suffering under oppressive heat and warm weather.

Monkey's Wedding: *Noun*
Rain and sunshine happening at the same time.

Ninguid: *Noun*
Snowy. Blanketed in snow.

Nithered: *Verb*
From Hull meaning to shiver as you are bone-chillingly cold.

Plothering: *Adjective*
The sound of it chucking it down with rain and the droplets hitting the ground.

Ponommerins: *Noun*
The name for light, fleecy clouds that dapple the sky.

Rawky: *Adjective*
Damp, foggy, and a little bit chilly.

Roke: *Noun*
A fog that rises in the evening off marshes and water meadows.

Snell: *Adjective*
Describes the keen biting cold.

Spindrift: *Noun*
The salty spray blown from the crests of a wave.

Stott / Stotting: *Verb*
From the North East of England when it is raining so hard it sounds like rocks are falling from the sky.

Sun-Wake: *Noun*
Rays from the sun reflect on the sea.

Twitterlight: *Noun*
   An old word for twilight.

Umbriphilous: *Adjective*
   Being fond of the shade.

Withering: *Adjective*
   Intense and scorching heat.

Wuthering: *Adjective*
   A   strong   wind   that   roars.

Wealth

Avidulous: *Adjective*
Being somewhat greedy.

Fornale: *Verb*
To pledge or spend money before you have it.

Lickpenny: *Noun*
Something that uses up large amounts of money.

Nuppence: *Noun*
To have no money. To be skint.

Pinchfart: *Noun*
A Miser is a person who hoards wealth and spends as little money   as   possible.

World of Work

Arsle: *Verb*
To not make any progress or move backwards on a project.

A fit of the Clevers: *Verb*
That sudden spurt of activity when you notice the time and how much you have left to do.

Boondoggle: *Noun*
A wasteful, unnecessary or fraudulent project that is continued due to extraneous policy, political motivations or merely as a means of looking busy.

Catchfart: *Noun*
An insult for anyone who sucks up to the boss.

Causey-webs: *Noun*
A person who neglects his/her work to hang out on the street outside.

Clusterfuck: *Noun*
A disastrously or deliberately mishandled situation or undertaking.

Empleomania: *Noun*
A manic compulsion to hold public office at any cost.

Eye-servant: *Noun*
A person who only works when the boss is looking.

Facienda: *Noun*
Something that needs to be done.

Forswunk: *Adjective*
To be exhausted from too much work.

Niffle-naffling: *Noun*
Ignoring the important stuff and instead dilly-dallying at work.

Nikehedonia: *Noun*
The pleasure that comes from the anticipation of success.

Noggle: *Verb*
An old dialect word for just about achieving something with difficulty.

Owl Jacket: *Noun*
When you leave your jacket on your office chair, but you are in fact out of the office skiving.

Ploiter: *Verb*
To work ineffectively.

Perendinate: *Verb*
To put something off until the day after tomorrow.

Procaffeinating: *Noun*
When you put everything off until you've had at least one mug of coffee.

Quiddling: *Verb*
To focus on the small tasks to delay doing the bigger tasks.

Roorback: *Noun*

A false and damaging report is circulated for political effect, usually about a candidate seeking office.

Spuddle: *Verb*

To work feebly and ineffectively because you haven't woken up properly yet or you're daydreaming.

Verschlimmbesserung: *Noun*

A German word for an improvement that only makes things worse.

Whindling: *Verb*

When you put on a voice to convince your boss you are ill and cannot   work.

Wrong

Misdelight: *Noun*

Taking pleasure in something being wrong or incorrect.

Conclusion

So there you have it!

I hope you've enjoyed reading this book as much as I have writing it.

I hope you can take the joy of discovering new words and enjoy sharing these unusual words with your friends, work colleagues and family.

If you found this book useful or interesting, I'd be very grateful if you could leave a favourable review on Amazon.

References

8 Words to Kill Your Appetite "Borborygmus", "keck", and other words unsuitable for the dinner
   table. (2022, March 9). www.Merriam-Webster.Com/Words-at-Play/Dinner-
   Words-You-Didnt-Know-You-Needed.
   www.merriam-webster.com/words-at-play/dinner-words-you-didnt-know-you-needed

12 wonderful words we should all be using. (n.d.).
   www.Bbc.Co.Uk/Programmes/Articles/38YYPQdPbVwWsW6py mn3yR4/12-
   Wonderful-Words-We-Should-All-Be-Using. Retrieved June 15, 2022, from
   www.bbc.co.uk/programmes/articles/38YYPQdPbVwWsW6py mn3yR4/12-
   wonderful-words-we-should-all-be-using

Asprey, E. (n.d.). *Gubbins and mosey: Eight old words and their meanings.*
   www.Bbc.Co.Uk/Programmes/Articles/4ZF5ZzlZSqZ3SmxXby0 XTBm/Gubbins-
   and-Mosey-Eight-Old-Words-and-Their-Meanings.
   www.bbc.co.uk/programmes/articles/4ZF5ZzlZSqZ3SmxXby0X TBm/gubbins-
   and-mosey-eight-old-words-and-their-meanings

Blake, I. (2016, November 1). *Can YOU pronounce suaveolent? Countdown's Susie Dent*
   reveals the unusual foodie words that describe how your favourite treats taste.
   www.Dailymail.Co.Uk/Femail/Food/Article-
   3889770/Countdown-s-Susie-
   Dent-Reveals-Unusual-Words-ve-NEVER-Heard-Way-
   Eat.Html. Retrieved June 15,
   2022, from www.dailymail.co.uk/femail/food/article-3889770

Brandreth, G. (2019, July 31). *From bang-a-bonk to cold turkey - it pays to increase your*
   word power.
   www.Gylesbrandreth.Net/Blog/2019/7/31/Dfq0cerehvh00ag2b
   nn0a6x282aqbq.
   Retrieved   June   15,   2022,   from
   www.gylesbrandreth.net/blog/2019/7/31

Burn, beck and burble: 11 words for water. (n.d.).
   www.Bbc.Co.Uk/Programmes/Articles/3SGbnCkR0fHKRGFDBF
   2vdZb/BurnBeck
   -and-Burble-11-Words-for-Water.
   www.bbc.co.uk/programmes/articles/3SGbnCkR0fHKRGFDBF2
   vdZb/burn-beck-
   and-burble-11-words-for-water

Crystal, D. (2015). *The Disappearing Dictionary: A Treasury of Lost English Dialect Words*
   (Main Market Ed.). Macmillan UK.

The Curious and Little-Known Slang Terms Found in Modern Britain.
   (n.d.).
   Https://Interestingliterature.Com/2016/12/the-Curious-and-
   Little-Known-Slang-

Terms-Found-in-Modern-Britain/.
www.interestingliterature.com/2016/12

Dent, S. (n.d.-a). *Something Rhymes With Purple.*
www.Globalplayer.Com/Podcasts/42KqGt/. Retrieved June 15, 2022, from
www.globalplayer.com/podcasts/42KqGt/

Dent, S. (n.d.-b). *Susie Dent's Top Tens: 10 Words to Describe Office Co-Workers.*
Https://Whynow.Co.Uk/Read/Susie-Dents-Top-Tens-10-Words-to-Describe-Office
Co-Workers. Retrieved June 15, 2022, from https://whynow.co.uk/read/susie-dents-
top-tens-10-words-to-describe-office-co-workers

Dent, S. (2005, April 5). *Cherubimical, as used by Benjamin Franklin, describes someone who*
is a happy-drunk, with a tendency to go around hugging everyone.
[Tweet]. Twitter.
www.twitter.com

Dent, S. (2018, April 20). *How Countdown's Susie Dent is using Twitter to bring old words*
back to the fore.
www.Wiltshiretimes.Co.Uk/Leisure/Showbiz/16174037.Countdowns-
Susie-Dent-Using-Twitter-Bring-Old-Words-Back-Fore/.
Retrieved June 15, 2022,
from www.wiltshiretimes.co.uk/leisure/showbiz

Dent, S. (2020, December 23). *From 'confelicity' to 'quafftide', my alternative Christmas*
dictionary, reviving forgotten words.
Https://Inews.Co.Uk/Opinion/Alternative-

Christmas-Dictionary-806675. Retrieved June 15, 2022, from https://inews.co.uk/opinion/alternative-christmas-dictionary-806675

Dent, S. (2021a, September 13). *Countdown's Susie Dent reveals her favourite word is an old*
Yorkshire term - but have you ever heard it? Www.Yorkshirepost.Com.
Retrieved June 15, 2022, from www.yorkshirepost.co.uk/heritage-and-retro/heritage/countdowns-susie-dent-reveals-her-favourite-word-is-an-old-yorkshire-term-but-have-you-ever-heard-it-3380927

Dent, S. (2021b, November 22). *Words for the good politicians are hard to find in the*
Dictionary - Susie Dent. www.Scotsman.Com/News/Opinion/Columnists/Words-for-the-Good-Politicians-Are-Hard-to-Find-in-the-Dictionary-Susie-Dent-3466987.
Retrieved June 15, 2022, from www.scotsman.com/news/opinion/columnists/words-for-the-good-politicians-are-hard-to-find-in-the-dictionary-susie-dent-3466987

Dent, S. (2021c, December 26). *From Respair to Cacklefart.*
www.Theguardian.Com/Commentisfree/2021/Dec/26.
Retrieved June 15, 2022, from www.theguardian.com/commentisfree/2021/dec/26

Feeds. (2019, March 4). Futility Closet. Retrieved June 20, 2022, from
www.futilitycloset.com/2019/03/04/in-a-word-598/

Forsyth, M. (2013, October 9). *Mark Forsyth's top 10 lost words.*
www.Theguardian.Com/Books/Booksblog/2013/Oct/09/Mark-Forsyth-the-
Horologicon-Top-10-Lost-Words. Retrieved June 15, 2022, from
www.theguardian.com/books/booksblog/2013/oct/09/mark-forsyth-the-
horologicon-top-10-lost-words

Gollumpus. (n.d.). Https://Words.Fromoldbooks.Org/Grose-VulgarTongue/g/Gollumpus.Html. Retrieved June 15, 2022, from
https://words.fromoldbooks.org/Grose-VulgarTongue/g/gollumpus.html

Grose, F. (2015). *1811 Dictionary of the Vulgar Tongue: A Dictionary of Buckish Slang,*
University Wit, and Pickpocket Eloquence. (null ed.). CreateSpace Independent Publishing
Platform.

In praise of all the lovely words. (2021, August 3).
www.Mumsnet.Com/Talk/Pedants_corner/4313294-In-Praise-of-All-the-
Lovely-Words-on-Susie-Dents-Twitter-Feed. Retrieved June 15, 2022, from
www.mumsnet.com/talk/pedants_corner/4313294-In-praise-of-all-the-
lovely-words-on-Susie-Dents-twitter-feed

Jones, P. A. (2018, February 7). *Lanspresado (n.) the one member of a group of friends who*
never has money with them [17thC slang].
www.Haggardhawks.Com/Post/Lanspresado.
www.haggardhawks.com/post

Kenyon, G. (2015, November 2). *Ever feel unease that the natural environment around you is*
changing for the worse? There's a word for that.* www.Bbc.Com/Future/Article/20151030-Have-You-Ever-Felt-Solastalgia.
Retrieved June 15, 2022, from www.bbc.com/future/article/20151030-have-you-ever-felt-solastalgia

Lingoda Team. (2020, October 7). *Funny English Words.* https://Blog.Lingoda.Com/En/Funny-English-Words/. Retrieved June 15, 2022, from https://blog.lingoda.com/en/funny-english-words/

Lost for words: 14 expressions that have vanished. (n.d.). www.Bbc.Co.Uk/Programmes/Articles/2xL1gH6FcyCtYH2NM6 zYhTK/Lost-for-Words-14-Expressions-That-Have-Vanished. www.bbc.co.uk/programmes/articles/2xL1gH6FcyCtYH2NM6z YhTK/lost-for-words-14-expressions-that-have-vanished

McDonald, L. (2018, April 23). *LOST LEXICON Countdown language expert Susie Dent brings*
some old English words back to modern-day conversation.* www.Thesun.Ie/Tvandshowbiz/Television/2483312/Countdow n-Language-Expert-Susie-Dent-Brings-Some-Old-English-Words-Back-to-Modern-Day-Conversation/. Retrieved June 15, 2022, from www.thesun.ie/tvandshowbiz/television/2483312/countdown-language-expert-susie-dent-brings-some-old-english-words-back-to-modern-day-conversation/

McNally, F. (2020, September 26). *The Countdown lexicographer on a life-long love of*
    languages, accidental fame and why 'gobshite' isn't as Irish as we think.
    www.Irishtimes.Com/Life-and-Style/People/Susie-Dent-Jimmy-Carr-Is-Incredibly-
    Rude-to-Me-i-Took-It-as-a-Compliment-1.4356339.
    Retrieved June 15, 2022, from
    www.irishtimes.com/life-and-style/people

Percorari-McBride, K. (2015, October 15). *20 Brilliant English Words Time Forgot.*
    Https://Writingjourney.Co/Blog/20-Brilliant-English-Words-That-Time-Forgot/.
    Retrieved   June   15,   2022,   from
    https://writingjourney.co/blog/20-brilliant-english-words-that-time-forgot/

Perry, S. (2009, June 13). *Isle of Wight Words: Twickered.* Https://Onthewight.Com/Isle-of-
    Wight-Words-Twickered/. Retrieved June 15, 2022, from
    https://onthewight.com/isle-of-wight-words-twickered/

Poronkusema. (2020, July 7).
    Https://Thatsnotcanon.Com/Grandiloquentspodcast/Episode42. Retrieved June 15,
    2022,   from
    https://thatsnotcanon.com/grandiloquentspodcast/episode42

Puzzomous. (n.d.). www.Grandiloquentwordoftheday.Com/Single-Post/Puzzomous.
    Retrieved   June   15,   2022,   from
    www.grandiloquentwordoftheday.com/single-post

Quinion,   M.   (n.d.).   *Absquatulate.*
www.Worldwidewords.Org/Weirdwords/Ww-Abs1.Htm.
Retrieved   June   15,   2022,   from
www.worldwidewords.org/weirdwords

Rosen, M. (n.d.-a). *From blunk to brickfielder: Our wonderful words for weather.*
www.Bbc.Co.Uk/Programmes/Articles/1gnSbXqRYSybzRHbCZX
03C3/from-Blunk-to-
Brickfielder-Our-Wonderful-Words-for-Weather.   Retrieved
June 15, 2022, from
www.bbc.co.uk/programmes/articles/1gnSbXqRYSybzRHbCZX
03C3/from-blunk-to-
brickfielder-our-wonderful-words-for-weather

Rosen, M. (n.d.-b). *Ittibitium, borborygmus, and Ba humbugi – 14 wonderful science words*
you've never heard of.
www.Bbc.Co.Uk/Programmes/Articles/1lVWXBgxX96Zf0TKV8t
3Jw1/Ittibitium-B
Borborygmus-and-Ba-Humbugi-14-Wonderful-Science-
Words-You-ve-Never-
Heard-Of.
www.bbc.co.uk/programmes/articles/1lVWXBgxX96Zf0TKV8t3
Jw1/ittibitium-
borborygmus-and-ba-humbugi-14-wonderful-science-
words-you-ve-never-
heard-of

Shaw, N. (2022, May 26). *Susie Dent lists 10 motoring phrases that are dying out, and 10 we*
need to learn. www.Cornwalllive.Com/Whats-on/Whats-on-
News/Susie-Dent-Lists-
10-Motoring-7130908.   Retrieved   June   15,   2022,   from
www.cornwalllive.com/whats-

on/whats-on-news/susie-dent-lists-10-motoring-7130908

Smith, L. (2020, October 4). *Year of the Mubble-Fubbles.* Sundaypost.Com. Retrieved June
15, 2022, from www.sundaypost.com

Sugden, M. (2022, January 28). *Pardon my French.* www.Heraldscotland.Com/News/19878920.Issue-Day-Pardon-French-Britains-
Endangered-Sayings/. Retrieved June 15, 2022, from
www.heraldscotland.com/news/19878920.issue-day-pardon-french-britains-
endangered-sayings/

Time to bitch the pot? (2018, June 12). Https://Writingcooperative.Com/Time-to-Bitch-
the-Pot-the-Victorian-Tea-Party-Slang-We-Need-to-Revive-73216b28d7fa.
Retrieved June 15, 2022, from https://writingcooperative.com/time-to-bitch-the-
pot-the-victorian-tea-party-slang-we-need-to-revive-73216b28d7fa

To Drown the Millar. (2011, August 3). Oxford Reference. Retrieved June 15, 2022, from
www.oxfordreference.com/view/10.1093/oi/authority.20110803095731859

Top 10 rare and amusing insults. (2020, April 20). Www.Merriam-Webster.Com. Retrieved
June 15, 2022, from www.merriam-webster.com/words-at-play/top-10-rare-and-
amusing-insults-vol-1

Trewhela, L. (2020, August 9). *The best weird and wonderful Cornish phrases to drop into*
conversation. www.Cornwalllive.Com/News/Cornwall-News/Best-Weird-Wonderful-
Cornish-Phrases-4394458. Retrieved June 15, 2022, from
www.cornwalllive.com/news/cornwall-news

Woode, D. (2020, February 22). *Susie Dent on swearing, social media and the influence of*
slang on the English language. Https://Inews.Co.Uk/Inews-Lifestyle/People/Susie-
Dent-Countdown-Interview-Swearing-Social-Media-Slang-400522. Retrieved June
15, 2022, from https://inews.co.uk/inews-lifestyle/people/

A writer's anthology of words and other writerly things. (2019, December 26).
www.Bookword.Co.Uk/Tag/Something-Rhymes-with-Purple/. Retrieved June 15,
2022, from www.bookword.co.uk/tag/something-rhymes-with-purple/

Printed in Great Britain
by Amazon

82536464R00058